COMPOSER SHOWCASE

HAL LEONARD STUDENT PIANO LIBRARY

LATE-INTERMEDIATE PIANO SOLOS

# Songs Without Words

## NINE CHARACTER PIECES FOR PIANO SOLO

### BY CHRISTOS TSITSAROS

*In Loving Memory of George Arvanitakis*

## CONTENTS

2 A Winter Fable

5 Arabesque (Autumn Storms)

9 Scherzo (Sledding)

14 Searching

18 Mirage

22 On The Wings Of A Song

26 Milonga De Los Niños

30 Sounds Of The Rain

36 Love's Sorrow

40 Notes From The Composer

I wish to express my deep appreciation and gratitude to Dr. Margaret Otwell for her idea to group these pieces into a collection under the title *Songs Without Words*, and for her encouragement and precious advice.

—Christos Tsitsaros

Edited by Margaret Otwell

ISBN 978-0-634-07843-9

HAL•LEONARD®
CORPORATION

7777 W. BLUEMOUND RD. P.O. BOX 13819 MILWAUKEE, WI 53213

In Australia Contact:
**Hal Leonard Australia Pty. Ltd.**
22 Taunton Drive P.O. Box 5130
Cheltenham East, 3192 Victoria, Australia
Email: ausadmin@halleonard.com

Visit Hal Leonard Online at
**www.halleonard.com**

# A Winter Fable

Christos Tsitsaros

Andantino (♩ = 116)

poco rit.

***p*** *a tempo*

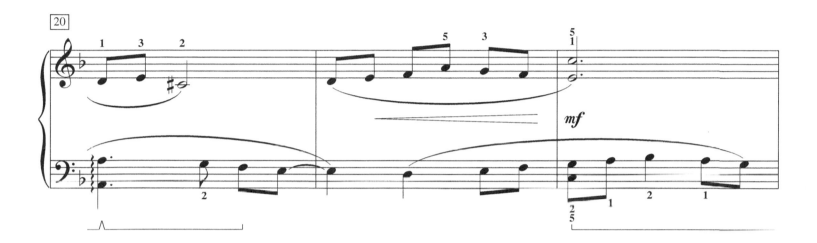

*mf*

*poco rit.*

*a tempo*

***mp***

*poco marcato il canto*

*simile*

poco rit.　　a tempo　　espressivo

espressivo e molto rit.

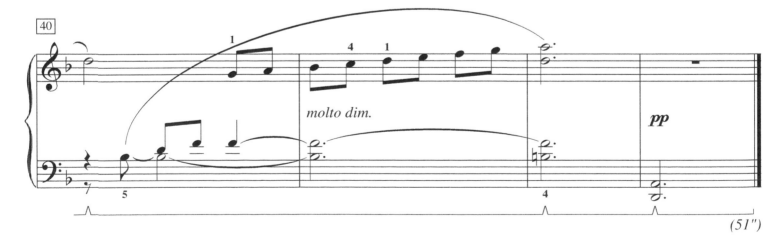

molto dim.　　pp

(51")

4

# Arabesque
### (Autumn Storms)

Christos Tsitsaros

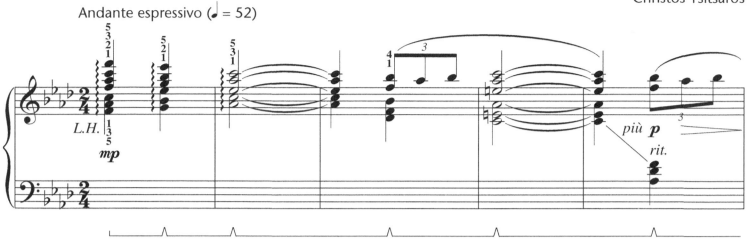

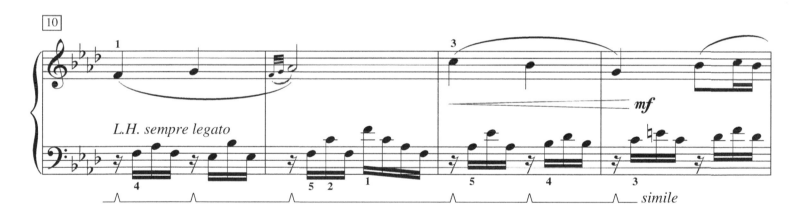

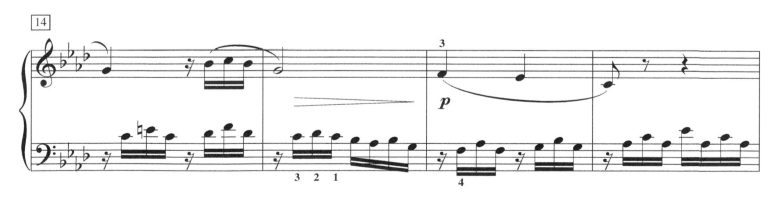

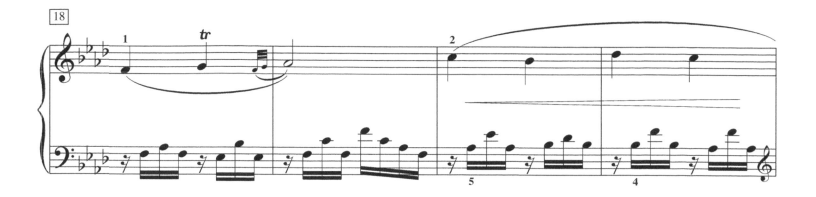

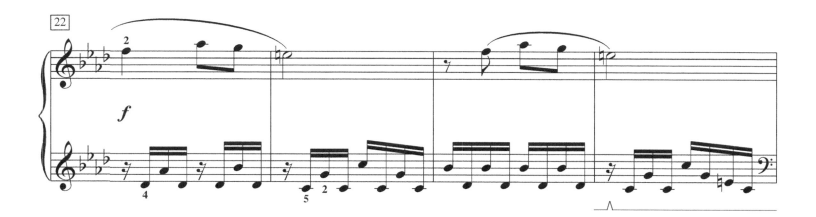

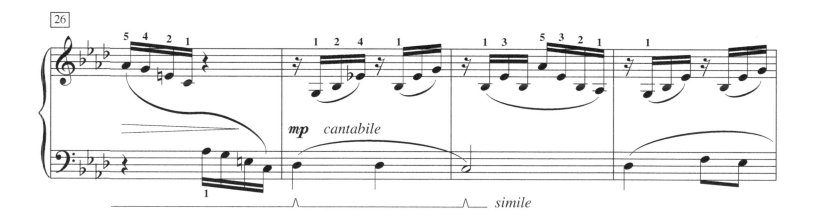

*assai:* quite

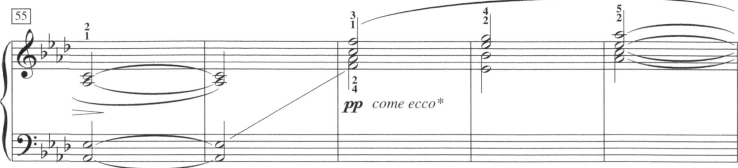

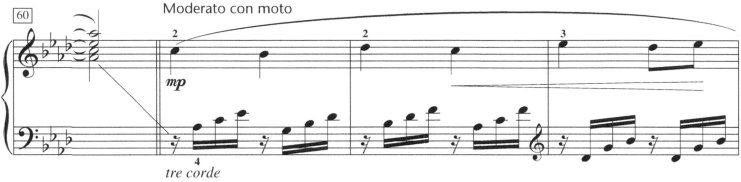

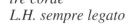

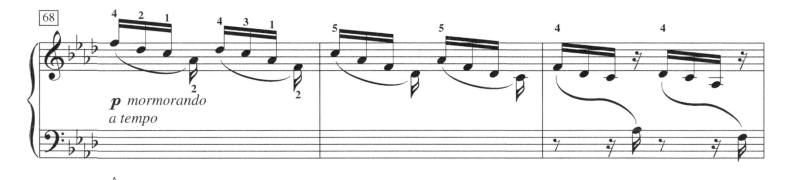

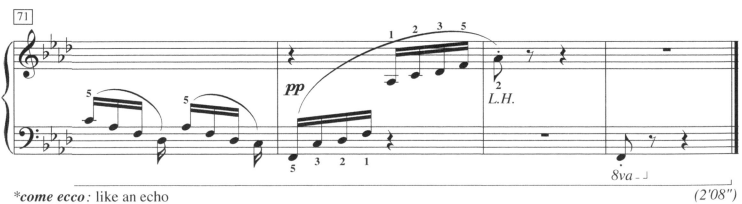

*come ecco*: like an echo

(2'08")

# Scherzo
## (Sledding)

Christos Tsitsaros

Allegretto grazioso (♩. = 84-88)

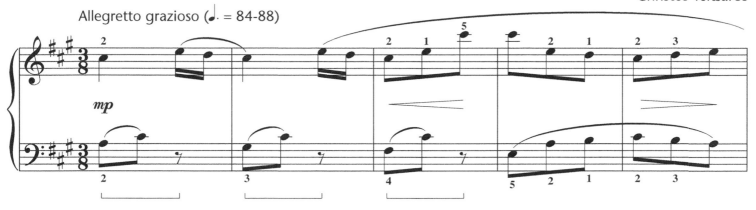

*poco cresc.*

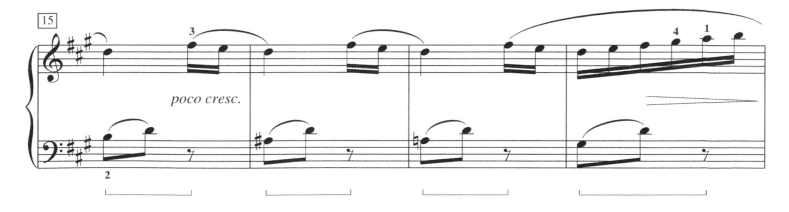

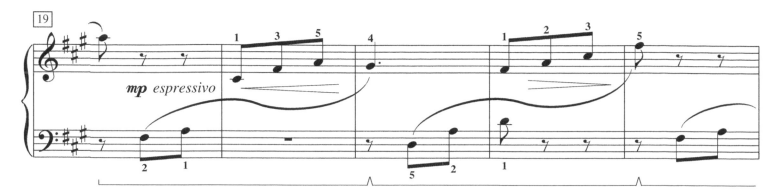

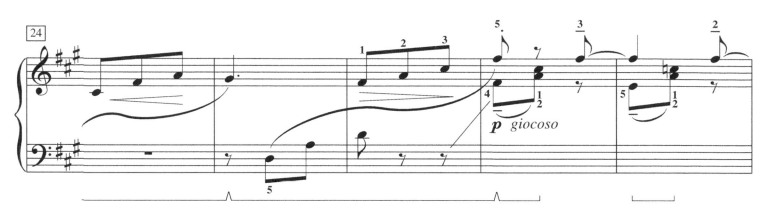

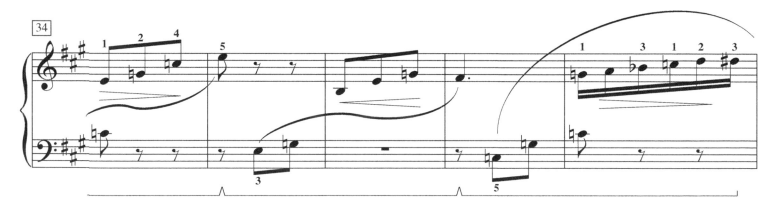

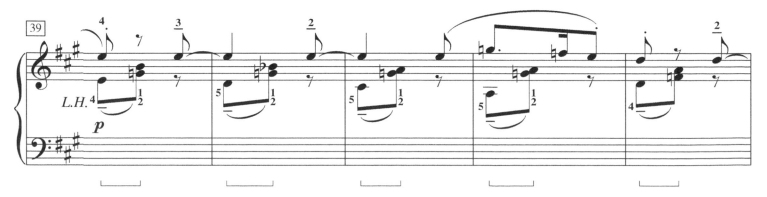

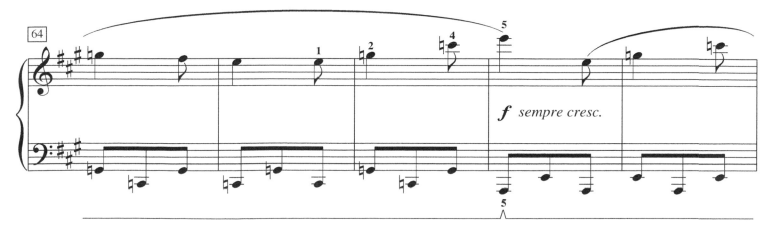

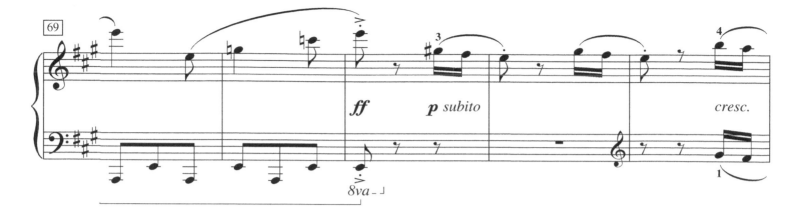

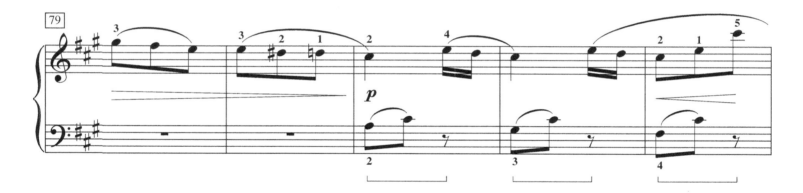

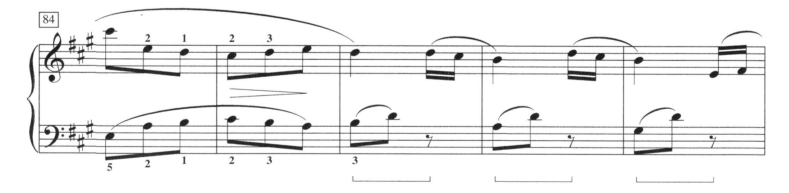

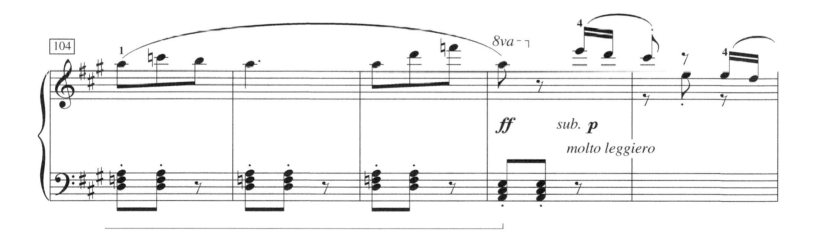

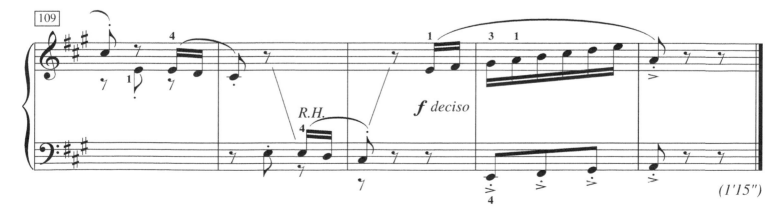

(1'15")

# Searching

Christos Tsitsaros

Allegretto inquieto (♩. = 86-92)

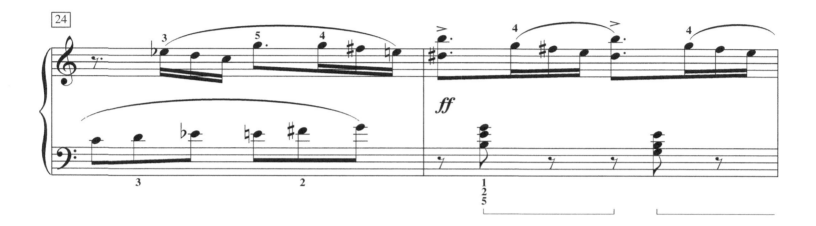

16

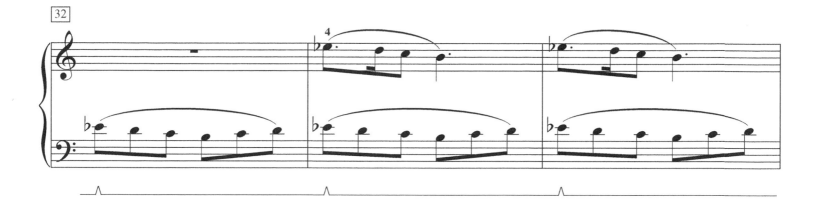

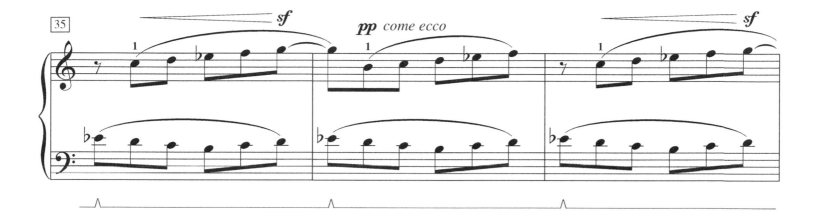

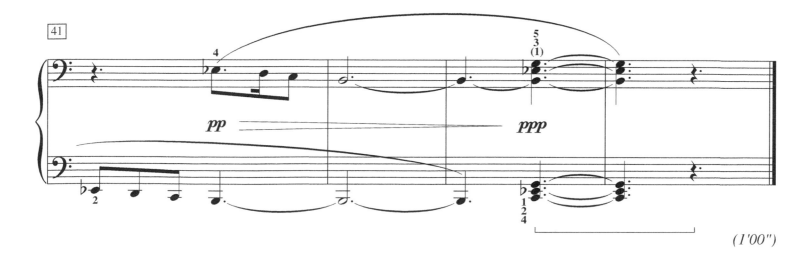

*(1'00")*

# Mirage

Christos Tsitsaros

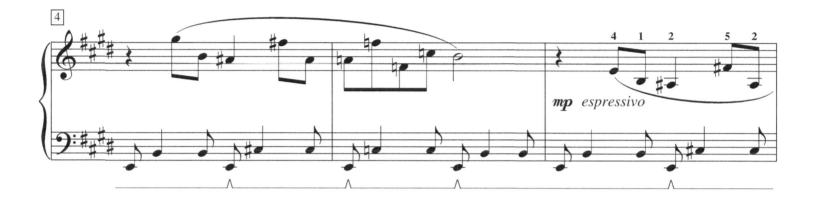

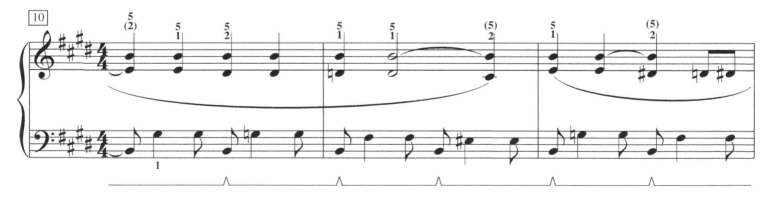

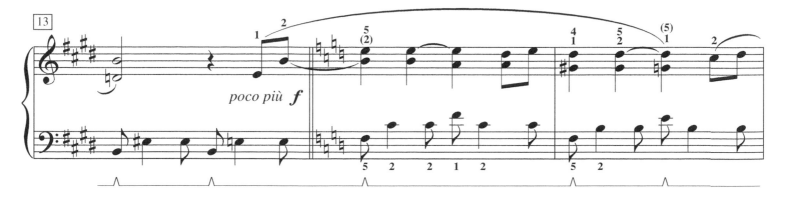

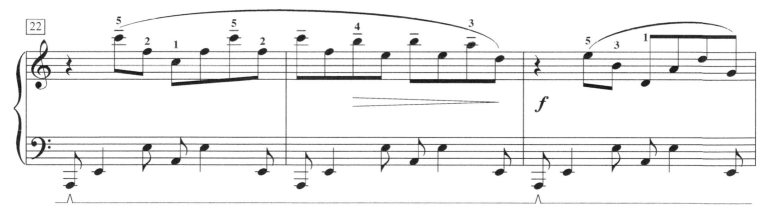

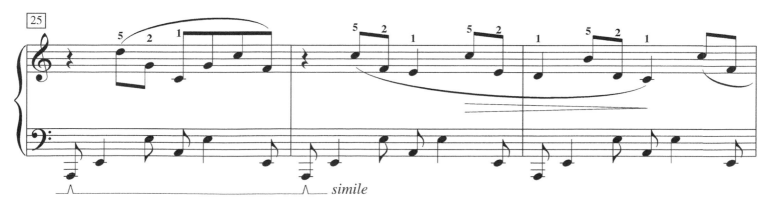

Tempo primo, molto tranquillo

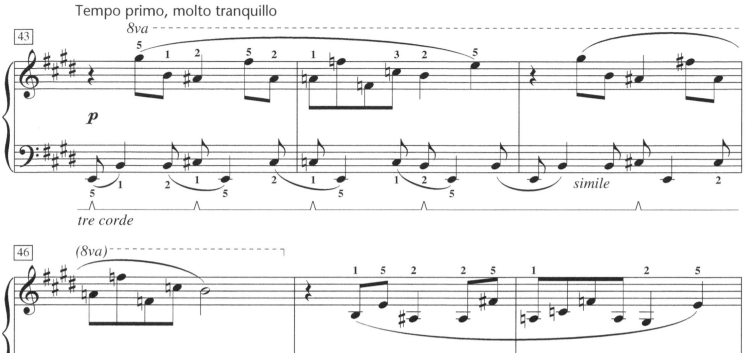

*poco a poco meno mosso al fine*

*sempre dim.*

*una corda al fine*

*morendo*

(2'11")

# On The Wings Of A Song

Christos Tsitsaros

Allegro con anima (♩ = 112-126)

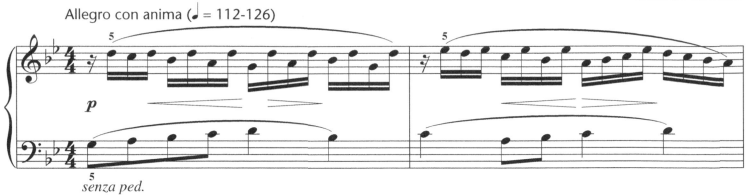

senza ped.

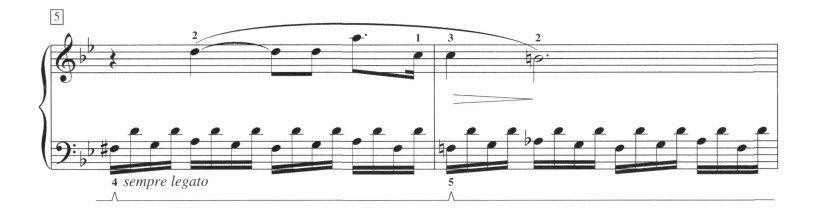

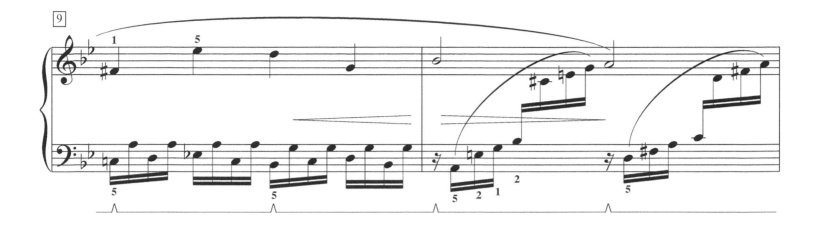

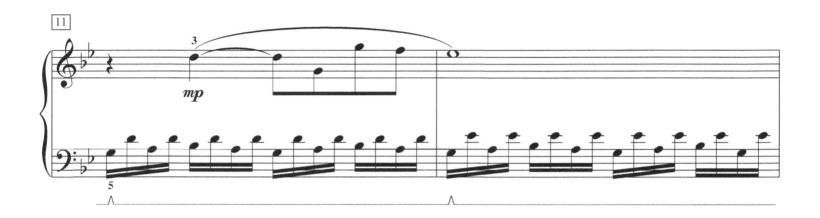

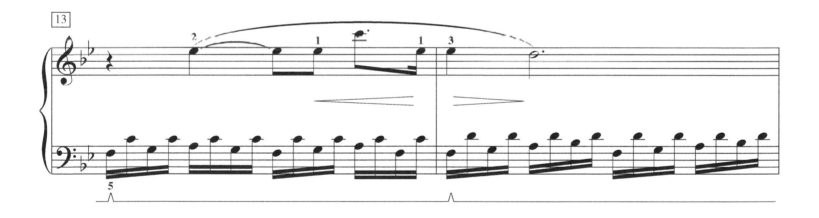

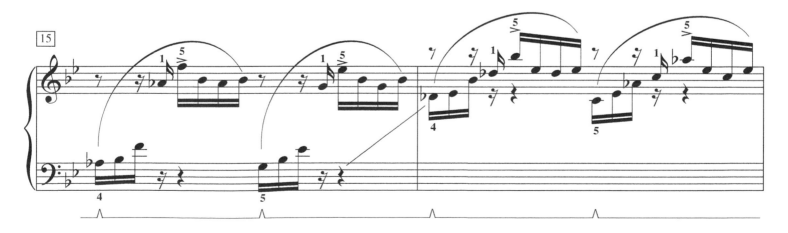

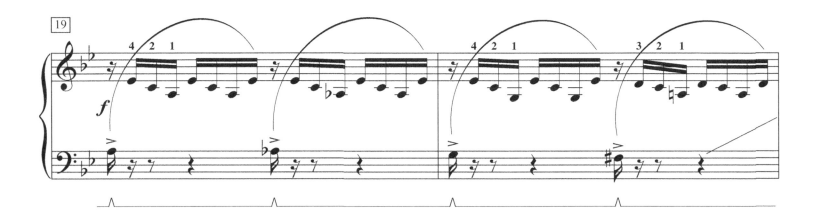

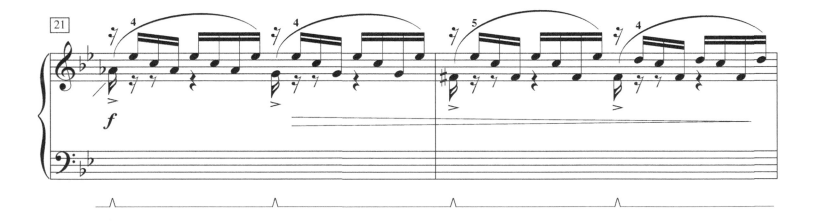

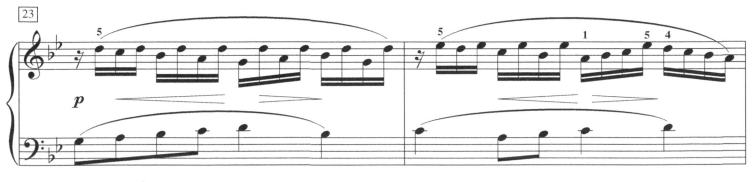

_senza ped._

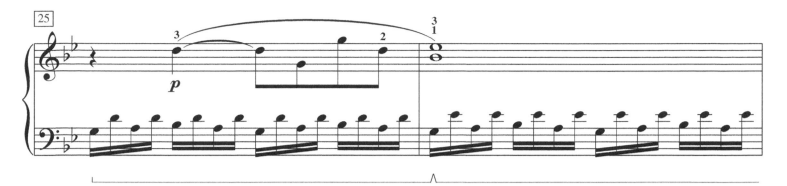

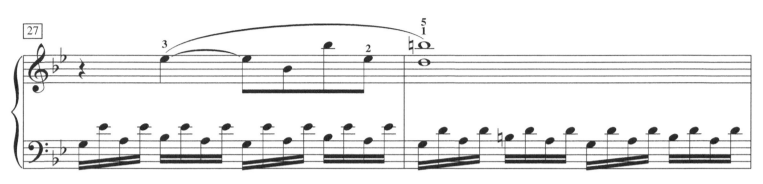

_simile_

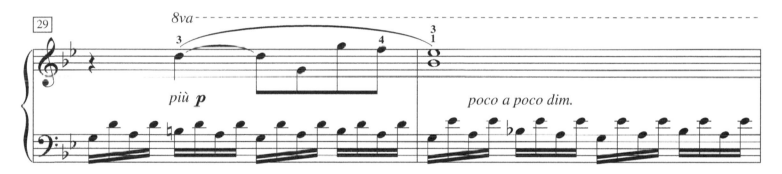

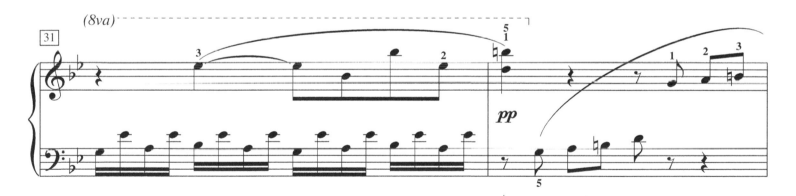

_(1"00")_

# Milonga De Los Niños

### (Dance Song Of The Children)

Christos Tsitsaros

Vivace e molto ritmico (♩ = 84-88)

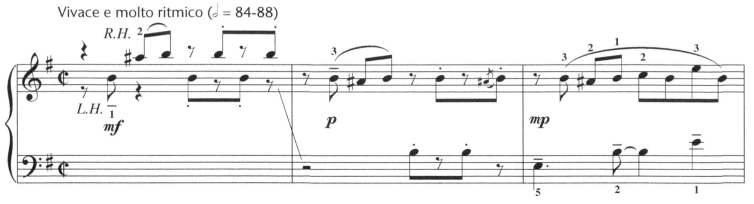

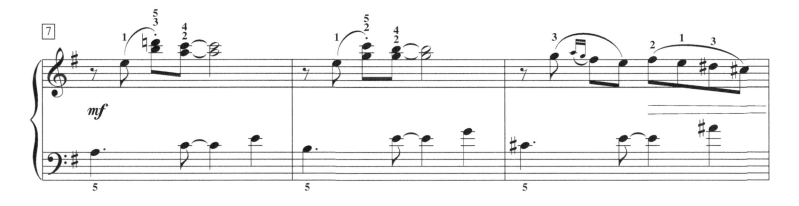

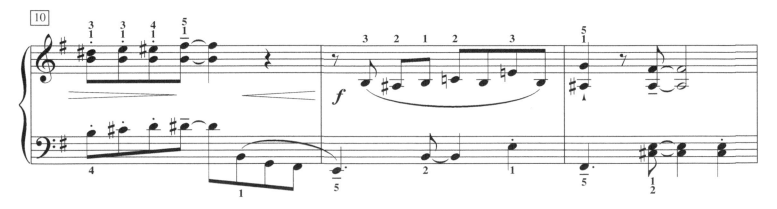

26

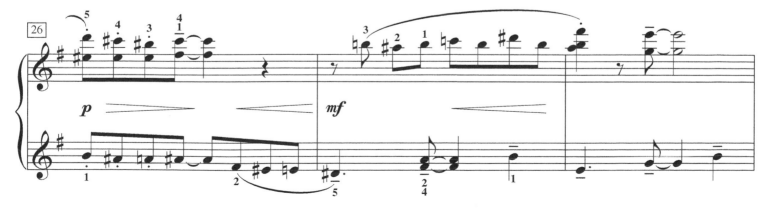

27

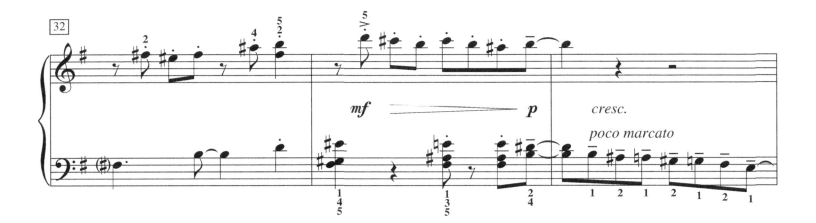

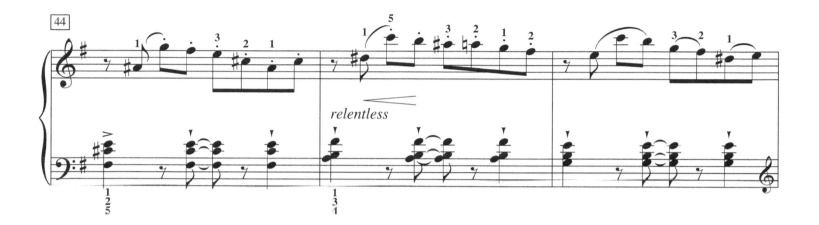

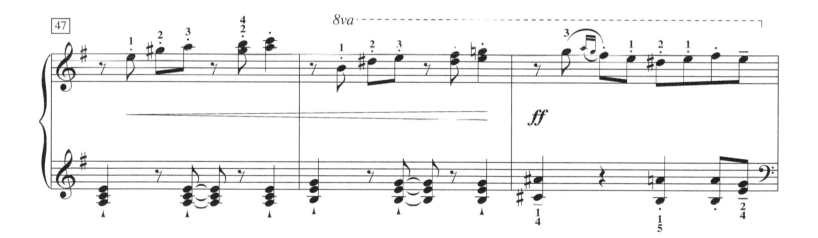

# Sounds Of The Rain

Christos Tsitsaros

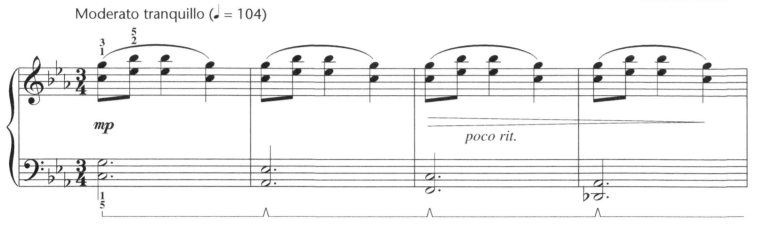

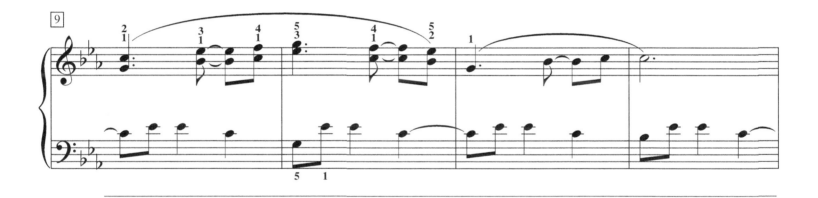

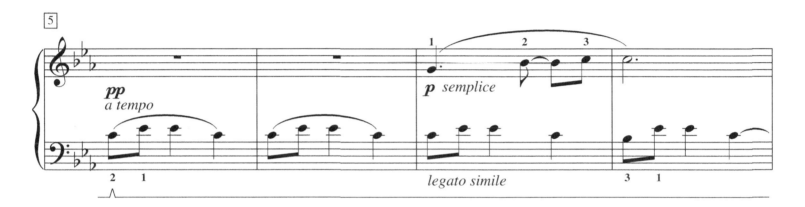

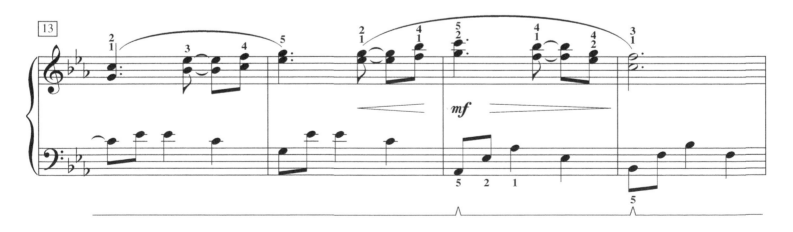

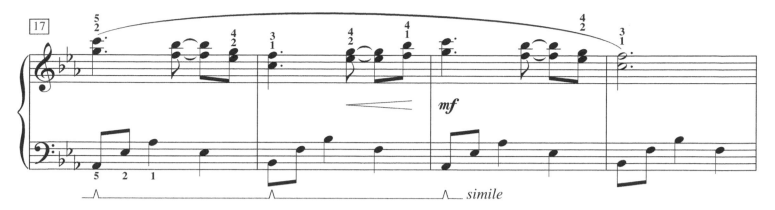

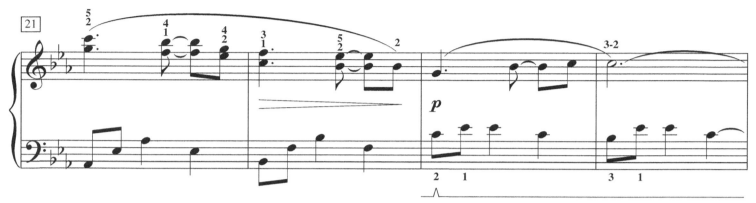

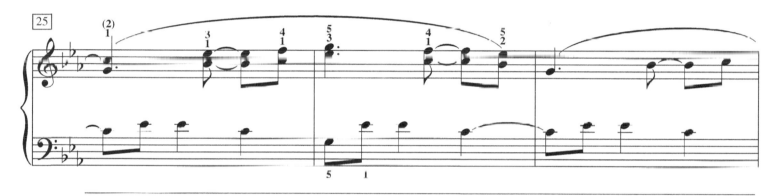

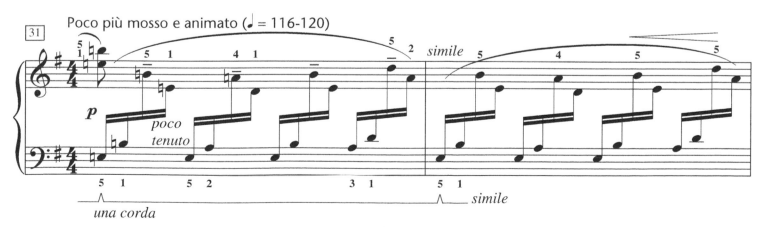

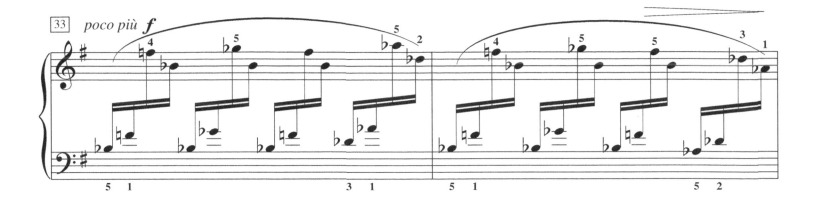

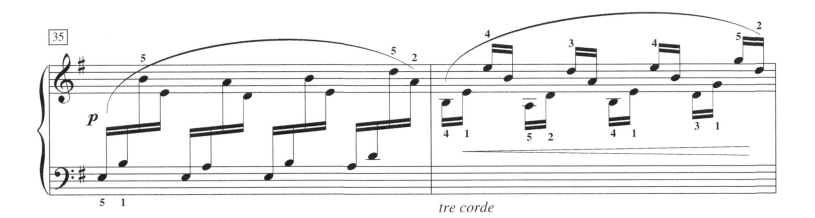

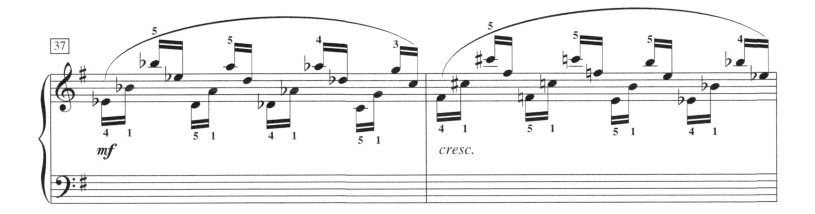

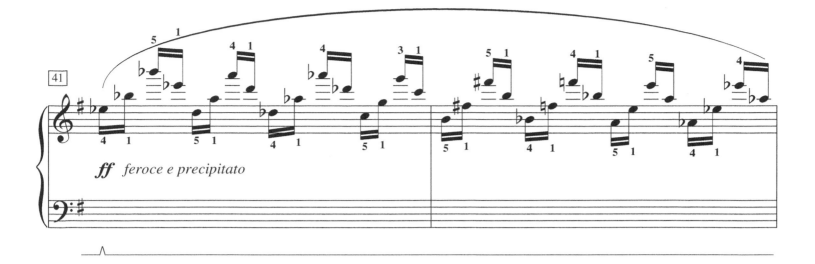

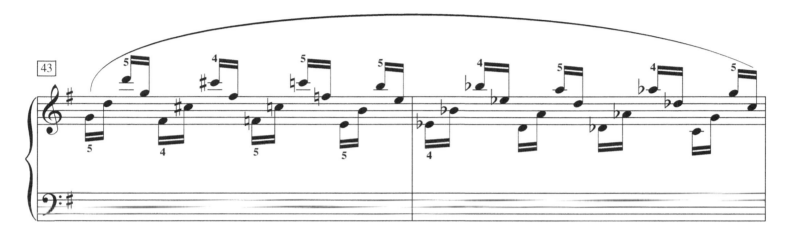

*poco a poco dim. e calando\**

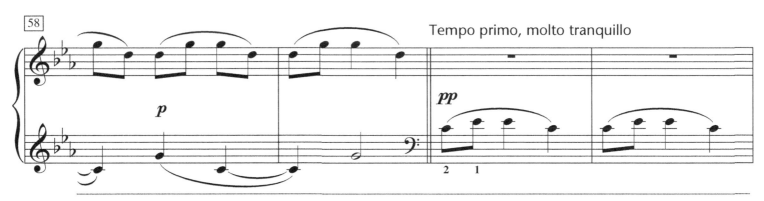

Tempo primo, molto tranquillo

*pp*

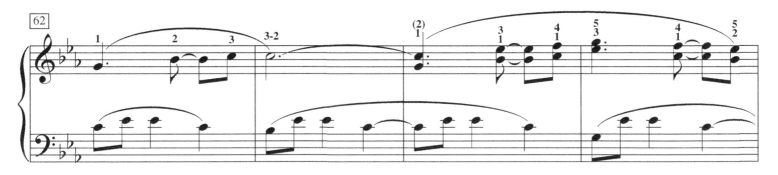

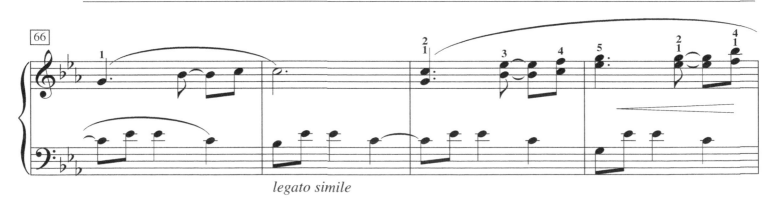

*legato simile*

**\*calando:** dying away

Poco più lento

*slentando: becoming slower

(2'08")

35

# Love's Sorrow

Christos Tsitsaros

Molto moderato, teneroso ($\bullet$. = 72)

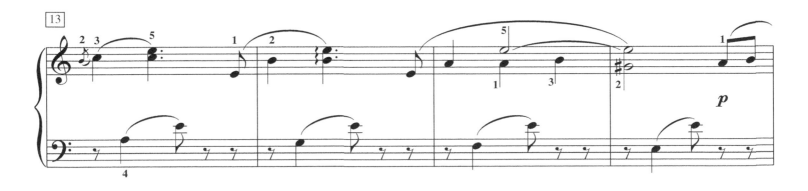

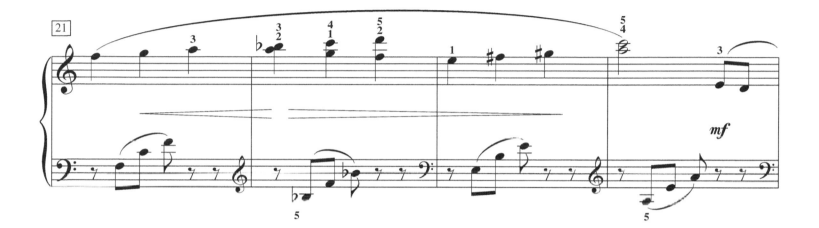

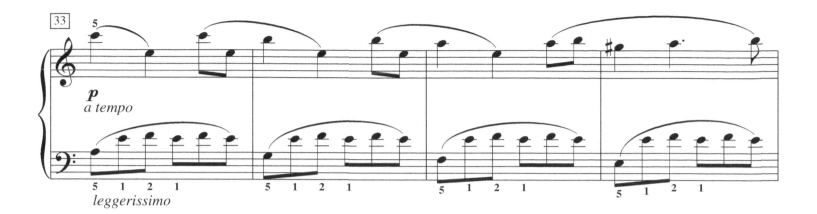

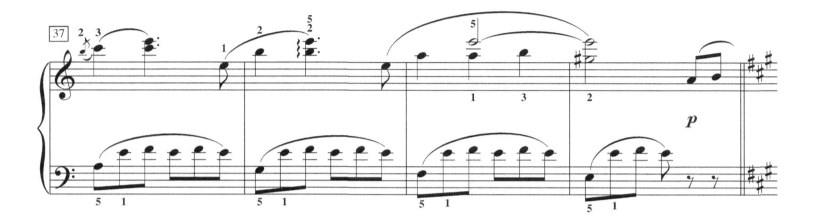

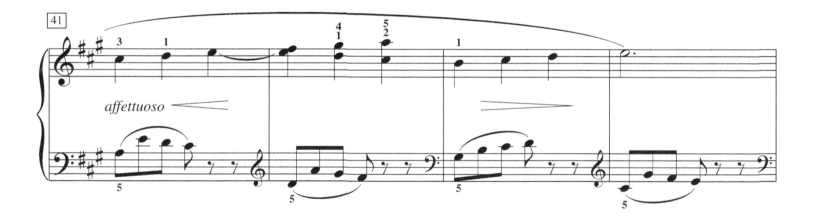

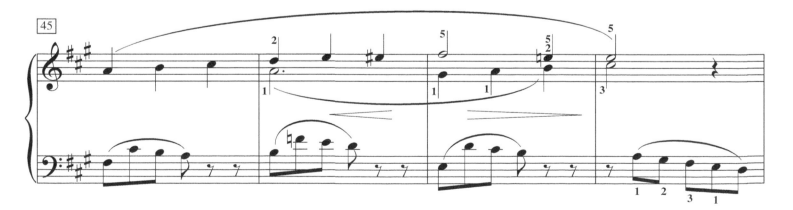

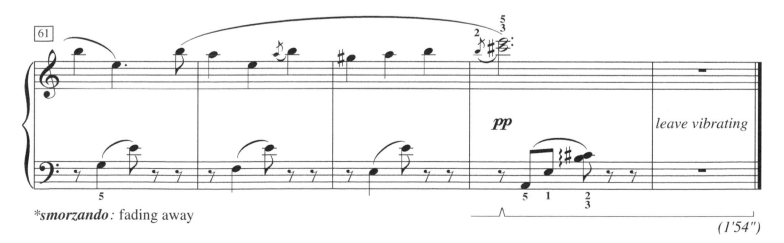

*smorzando*: fading away

(1'54")

# Notes From The Composer

The *Songs Without Words* aim at introducing piano students to the kinds of challenges that are present in the late-intermediate and early-advanced literature of the great piano masters, composers such as Grieg, Chopin, Schumann, Scriabin, Rachmaninoff, Debussy, and Prokofiev. In spite of the multitude of wonderful materials for the student player (Burgmüller, Heller, Bertini—to name a few), I find a definite gap between the musical level in them and the degree of refinement and sophistication inherent in a Chopin mazurka or an intermezzo by Brahms.

With this in mind, I have tried to address here a set of technical and musical problems. These include:
- the broadening of the dynamic range (*Sounds Of The Rain, Mirage, Searching*)
- a gradual, careful sense of phrasing (*Winter Fable, Arabesque*)
- the balance between the hands (*Winter Fable, Arabesque*)
- the lightness of the finger-work in combination with the stability of the tempo (*Scherzo, On The Wings Of A Song*)
- the projection of the larger line of the work
- the correct and agile use of the pedals

Several of the pieces encourage the development of *rubato* and tempo relations, concepts which form an integral part of the advancing pianist's preparation:
- *Sounds Of The Rain* presents sections of different time signatures that are bridged together through slight tempo fluctuations.
- *Mirage* and *Love's Sorrow*, through their internal imagery, lead the student to exploit the expressive possibilities of a tasteful *rubato*.
- A very rigorous rhythmic precision, coupled with the mastery of different articulations played simultaneously is required in *Searching, Sledding*, and *Milonga De Los Niños*.
- In *Love's Sorrow*, the metric structure opposes the melodic gesture. The right-hand motive should preserve the metrical accents of the 6/8 time signature, never lapsing into 3/4, despite the look of the notation. The music should be perceived in groups of three eighth-notes at all times.

The inspiration for *Songs Without Words* stems from various poetic images, ranging from external to personal and abstract. *Winter Tale* speaks of places immersed in mystery and of hearts that unite after a long separation. In *Arabesque*, one can hear the echo of an old hollow bell ringing and feel the autumn breezes drawing their playful arabesques. *Sledding* is a musical impression of playful sounds and laughter, with a winter landscape as the backdrop. There is no external image for *Searching*. Rather, it is about a state of the soul, a song without words in the real sense, since language cannot adequately express the emotions contained within it. Alongside the image of a caravan that traverses the desert, *Mirage* reflects the never-ending journey of self-realization and the final reconciliation with oneself. The long melodic line in *On The Wings Of A Song* is carried over a soaring, fast-moving accompaniment expressing the happiness that mixes with impatience when one is hopeful, driven, and inspired. Though it begins as an innocent dance, *Milonga De Los Niños* leads to a powerful conclusion through passionate rhythmic accents and an engaging contrapuntal texture. *Sounds Of The Rain* is another of those pieces where the music generates the emotions. It is about the kind of relief we experience when a light rain falls in the early evening, and the mystery and wonder it generates as it grows stronger. The memory of tender moments melts away in the final phrases of *Love's Sorrow*, not unlike the flame of a dying candle that leaves behind it a bittersweet smell.

It should be noted that the key scheme of this collection forms an arch through a D Minor ninth chord, ascending in thirds from the root to the ninth, then descending from the ninth down to the fifth. The pieces can be performed at various levels of advancement, as their emotional content far exceeds their technical demands. It is hoped that the more mature player, as well as the student pianist, will find satisfaction in studying these intimate, personal pieces.